Heart Less

ALSO BY CARLEY MOORE

Panpocalypse
The Not Wives
16 Pills
Portal Poem
The Stalker Chronicles

Heart Less

POEMS

CARLEY MOORE

INDOLENT BOOKS

© 2024 Carley Moore
All Rights Reserved
book design: adam b. bohannon
Book editor: Michael Broder
Cover photo: Matt Longabucco

www.indolentbooks.com
Indolent Books
209 Madison Street
Brooklyn, NY 11216

ISBN: 978-1-945023-33-0

Special thanks to Epic Sponsor Megan Chinburg
for helping to fund the production of this book.

For Milton Kessler

CONTENTS

I. TENDER HOOKS

My Pretty	3
Code	5
Quiet Night	6
Transplant	8
Proxy	9
Kid	10
Demiurge	11
Top Stories	12
Tender Hooks	13
Sick Day	14
Graft	16
Parachute	17
Pushy	18
Ice	19
Present Tense	20
Soft Apocalypse	21
The Skiff	23
The Fisherman's Wife	24

II. PORTAL POEM

Portal Poem	27

III. FUTURE PERFECT

Lexapro Poem	47
Future Perfect	48
Winter Wonderland	50
Mourning Instructions	51
My Second Husband	52

Apology	53
Do You Have a Boyfriend?	54
Lion or Lamb	55
Early Morning	56
Frankincense	58
Mother's Day Poem	59
Quickie	61
Mediation	63
Specimen	64
My Coven	65
Post Bowie	67
Rituals for Saying Good-Bye to Things that Never Quite Were	69
Heart Less	71

I.
TENDER HOOKS

My Pretty

Hard heart,
you need a harder hat.
Or a straightjacket.
Or a shell.
Or the perfect pill.

Artful meme.
You run after
even shadow men.
A full beard.
A tooth pick.
Achy.
Breaky.

At night,
you're all hag,
feathered and clawing
at the nest of my ribs,
hand-standing on my chest.
All press.
No give.

Heart, I told you
to get harder.
Muscle up.
Hire a trainer.

This ache won't do.
These sinews strain.

This stretched cartilage.
This hurting casts a cloud
    over the stroller's crummy seat.
And it makes the curtains cry,
the plants dry out, the books stupid.

I catch a glimpse of you
in the drugstore window
your breaking-news beat—
all deft chambers and purple ventricles.
Hard matter, I think
as I turn my head and watch you go.

Code

It's the way of cells to divide.

In the YouTube videos
    I see my own long divisions.

This nuclear split makes two daughters.

The new cells rub up against each other,
    share a wall, and vibrate with proximity.

If the kernel of life is to separate and iterate,
    then why do I cling to wrecks?

These ossified hulls.
    This cleaving.
        Barnacle. Bivalve.

I'll feel along the shared wall of the one who left.

There's a code there,
    now just to crack it.

Quiet Night

I draw the shades,
   shut her door,
      descend into the computer screen,
      and wish it were otherwise.

Do you know the dimensions of my apartment?
The 150 watt bulb in the living room?
The linoleum that curls up in the corners of the kitchen?
The dining room framed by books?
This morning, my landlord,
   the mother of three teenagers,
      said to me on the walk to the subway,
"It's better if you just accept that life is hard."

I spend 45 minutes wishing I could do what I need to do faster.
I move between Facebook, Gmail, and my university account.
I respond to no one.
I look at winter coats on-line, but I don't buy one.
I make a lesson plan.
I read the essays I assigned and text my mother,
   who calls me back in response.
I don't pick up.
I spread out my orange yoga mat and do a couple of sun salutations
      until the cat sits between my pressed-down palms and bats at my hair.

When I get into bed the sheets are cold.
There's a pattern on the wall, a siren outside,
   and two tipsy voices from the bar on the corner.
One says, "You're an ass," and the other says, "Buy me a drink."

The pillow is wet.

I tell myself there's supposed to be missing and waiting, boredom too.

I move in increments and fractions.

I am several places to the right of the decimal point.

I slow the room and call it stuck.

Transplant

My hag heart is fatty, marbled,
working hard at not working.
"Do you know how many of us
have died on the treadmill,
the elliptical, the Stairmaster?
Lots," it says, all flip, all right about it.

On good days, I think I'll get a new heart.
Lay a redder, faster, more pumpish one
on top of the old one, cast a spell and *voila!*
New surprising feeling!
Hard hurting animal!
Pretty now—veined up and thawed out.

Proxy

On the eve of my separation,
    she tells me to text her every day,
        "So I don't have to worry."

I've grown up to fail at what she raised me to do.
I was her small confidant, an eager untrained therapist.
I sat on the toilet while she took a bath.
We talked about my father—
    everything we could think of that was wrong with him—
        his weight, the underwear he left on the floor, his spitting rage.

My mother's fears for me are fixed
    over instant coffee and *The Weather Channel.*
"Who will take care of you?
Don't drive your car into a snowstorm.
Do you really have to fly?"

How hard it must be to have lost the girl
    who perched on the porcelain and took it all in.
The one who asked, "Yes?" and "What else did he do?"

Kid

Tiny traveler.
Persephone of weekends.

We make pizza, draw rainbows, and listen to the Pretenders album I
    bought
  at your school fair.
Kid my only kid
You look so small
You've gone so quiet.

In my twenties, I thought motherhood was collaborative art projects and
    mixed tapes.

At night, you turn like a sundial
  and press your feet into my back.

In the morning, you tell me about the dream.
   "I was alone in the forest.
   I ran, but the bear ate me anyway.
   Then you were there and we lived in the bear's mouth.
   It was hot and we couldn't get out."

"At least we were together," I offer and you say, "Mama, I know that
    already."

Demiurge

Shhhhhhhh.
    Flip the switch.
Let's book the trip.

At the reading.
    Demi-anxiety.

Maudlin chardonnay.
    Demi-fugue.

You sit with your kid.
    Say good-bye to your kid.

Two lives run alongside of each other.
    In one you sit alone in a faux-leather booth with a pen.
        In the other you are together like the other couples.

You don't separate your books
    and all of the accounts.

Ledgers.
    Jump!
Parenthesis.
    Swell!
Taxes.
    Whee!

Top Stories

The poet who hates you.
Your difficult cat.
The vet called him "obese," but "Isn't he just hungry?"
    you wanted to say, but didn't.
The BBC—9:30 am, certain and clipped.
The girls who have been kidnapped at school.
The threat of their rape.
Their mothers.

Your own girl.
In kindergarten they are
    learning to write persuasive letters.
Your girl wants to write about bullies, litter,
    and trampled flowers.
Jessa, who calls her a weirdo at lunch.

There's gossip about you.
    Maybe.

The girls become profile pictures.
    No one is doing anything about the stolen girls.

And let's be clear, this poem is not a thing.
It's a to-do list
    or a guilt record.

You are local, like your own girl.
    And that poet will always hate you.

Tender Hooks

Let's take our fat hearts to the bar.
There's a D.J. who's got that 90s show, we should go.

Let's stack feelings, smash them together.
Crush them until they're gone.

Let's rack shit up.
Spend it all on Victoria's Secret underwear and Blow Pops.

Let's get our little dogs and put them in baskets.
Ignore the yapping and the shit that comes through the wicker.

Let's not do the kindergarten applications.
Definitely we'll skip the gifted and talented test.

Let's hang our broken hearts side by side on meat hooks.
Wait for the butcher to come and turn us into choice cuts.

Sick Day

Last night I caught all of the barf
    in a Tupperware mixing bowl.

Today is a six-hour nap and a good *Finding Nemo* cry.
    Chicken nuggets for lunch and dinner.

They look like they're having brunch out there.
    The tree branches in the park are knuckled.

The radio plays tadpoles munching on a microphone.
"Shhhh, I can't hear them."

A book about the names of clouds and Anselm's *Sure Shot*.
    Ledge and surface.
        My cold hand in a sunny window.

A student hyperventilates in my apartment.
    She begs me not to tell.

The Post-it at the bottom of my purse says:
    Mammogram!
    Foot wart
    Glasses
There was sand too and an old cough drop.

I remember the garbage I forgot.
    The boat wedged between two trees.
    Newspapers that wrapped themselves around my shins.
    The stew of potato chip bags on the subway tracks.

A Home Depot cart piled high with curtain rods and picture frames.
Pregnancy jeans.

I am a husk or a seed pod.
    I molt.

I don't recognize my old body, but tether it to me anyway,
    and use it for shade.

Graft

My heart waits for the light to change.

The green field is so much bigger than I imagined. The grass is deeper too, more treacherous. And the island has cliffs, several rocky banks where I see myself slipping. Both landscapes are full of invading species—cicadas, purple loosestrife, and Japanese beetles.

There are lots of birds.
The hawk we stalk who lives on the library ledge.
Her babies.
The loud ones outside of my seventh floor window.

I get used to half the time—time elapsing, stretched out and bored with itself.

Desire is flattening, crushing even.
Desire walks me around and winds me up.
It's faceless.
A muscled back.
      His fingernails.
           The un-answered text.

The dictionary says it's surgery—one tissue on top of another.
    Cut, slit, splice, and wait.

Parachute

The dream's edges are gold flake and cypress.
    Remember the olive grove of those first bewildering fights?
And the Great Dane who herded us into our apartment
    without so much as a bark or a growl?
Those baleful, watery eyes.
Legs longer than mine.

There are no children, but I've brought my father,
    who complains about the lack of colored postcards in downtown
        Florence.

You kiss your new girlfriend.
You sit together in a giant orange armchair.
You do or do not know I'm watching.
No one is hounding you.
You're not tired anymore.

I wake myself up.
    Our daughter, asleep next to me.
She's taken her pajamas off,
    and her breath is mouthy.
She's naked and perfect, our only manifest.

You are your own planet now.
I no longer know your atmosphere or trip on your rocky landscape.
    I don't orbit you.

Good-bye twin.
Good-bye parachute.

Pushy

I don't need much, I think, *just a trip to the Pathmark,*
    this steak, these eggs.

We meet at the Guitar Center and then I buy you a sangria.

On the corner of 23rd and 8th you give me the limp hug
    of the no-longer-fucking.

We stand next to each other at all of the book parties.

The app is all push.

Ice

We squint to see ourselves.
    As hazy stars.
        As a distant moon.

"I'm thinking about you," she says on the walk to school.
    It's twenty degrees.
We wear hoods over our hats
    and scale the crusted, gray ice on each corner.
"That I'm going to be missing you."

Am I half a mom?
    I have a whole girl half the time.

I say we need a picture of me
    or a stuffed animal proxy.

My dumb problem solving.
    The fixer in me.

"I'm still sad," she says.

"I know.
    Me too."

Present Tense

I take the Peter Pan bus to Bucks County
    and for a night I stop counting bodies.

I sleep next to a wolf
    and because he's a wolf, there's no future conditional.
        But it's confusing because he also talks.

I dream I'm up for renewal
    and I've missed the deadline.
        My materials will be late, but I pretend otherwise.

It rains in the night.
    Sounds like acorns on the roof.
        Or squirrel paws.

The wolf says, "I had a nightmare, I thought you were dead."

His back is a picture window
    or a painting or a field.

I see lungs.
    Poison ivy leaves.
        The woman who throws her head back in ecstasy.

If we are the present tense then where do I stash the future?

Soft Apocalypse

In the future dream
    we live in the water-marked edges of Brooklyn.
Our building is vast and unknowable.
There are long lines for the elevators
    and large beds in the hallways serve as make-shift apartments.
        Well-made barges, candle-lit, but still a last resort.

I have two children.
The boy I lost in the fifth month is a real boy,
    standing next to my girl in the elevator line.

At the mouth of the elevator there's some confusion, a scuffle.
A neighbor tells me to go up without them.
She nods.
    "It's okay, they're safe," she says, and I agree.

My girl's face falls as the door shuts between us.
Something final.
Something lost.
We were not to separate!
How could I have forgotten?

I spend the rest of the dream searching the dim hallways,
    pulling on the arms of children who are not mine.
        "Have you seen them? They are seven. Twins."

The radio wakes me.
    Stops the future with its hard present.

In Nigeria, Boko Haram is using eight year-old-girls as suicide bombers.
  "Do they have a choice?" the BBC reporter burbles.

The cat cries.
I turn off the radio to wake her.
"Get up," I say, "We have to get up."

The Skiff

My heart is a skiff,
    pirated in swells.
You sail it.
You race it.
You win.

I rig up a tattered sail,
    and send out an S.O.S.
All is lost.
All is lost.

I see through squall.
I'm an icy gambit.

I dream big in the wolf's lair.
The shape of it is airport hangar.
The heat of it is hair dryer.
I stumble towards a nursery school.
There are kids outside of it—singing and shouting.
Their high voices are honey, Calypso, sirens, all of it.
I step onto the frozen river that moats their yard.
It splinters, groans, and opens up.

Underneath the ice is more ice.
Underneath the boat is more boat.
Underneath the heart is more heart.

The Fisherman's Wife

after Katsushika Hokusai

Longing is a swell dashed on a rock.

She sails her boat to the black deep and strips.
Asking for it.
    Waiting for it.
She stares into the bored sun.

It takes days, years.
He has long tentacles, watery eyes, and an embarrassingly large brain.
He flips the boat.
He pulls her down.
    Crest.
        Break.

She capsizes.
    Comes in waves.
She swallows ocean.
    Spits it back out.

She washes up onto the shore.
    She tells the whole village.

"I felt something.
I swam.
I had a spear and a net.
I caught a fish and I stared into his land-blind eyes
    and then I let him go."

II.
PORTAL POEM

Portal Poem

for Anne Boyer and Stacy Szymaszek

April is of uncertain origin
    Apru
    Aphrilis
    Aphrodite
    From the Latin, aperio, to bud

April is a deep portal
    The storm as it quits
        Thaw's garbage
            Heat tease

                * * *

He said, "I'm just a man, not a wolf."

I looked over my shoulder at the pile of mythologies
    underneath the stairs

They were bones now
    I'd licked them clean
        and sucked out the marrow.

                * * *

I stand in the sun
    squinting, desperate animal
        I eat the cheese grits with a spork

The wolf's mother was coming,
    so I gathered my clothes in a ball and left

I looked at the phone
    There were messages from some of my future ex husbands and wives
        They said, "You have a beautiful smile,"
            and "You are clearly a woman of light and talent."

At the co-parenting Seder we joked about the wives
    who took all of the furniture.
        "Ha," we said. "Ha."

And there were three girls in long white dresses, who skipped their dinners
    to read to us from workbooks about pharaohs, slaves,
        and an exodus without flour.

I left early to go to the movies.
    I cannot sit still.
    I cannot grade these essays
        because it is a stillness that had no effect.

Later, the woman on the subway platform yells,
    "I am hungry! Please feed me! I am hungry! Please feed me!"
        I give her my peanut butter frosted brownie and she stops.

* * *

"Your butt is a marshmallow pillow,"
    she says and punches it.

I don't feel anything.

I never know what's behind me.
    In college I failed as a bus girl.
        I couldn't maneuver the steak house labyrinth.
I dropped forks, glasses, and then a full tray of dishes.

In the bathroom we talk about the blood.
    "Ewwww," she says.

My phone chirps,
    "I'm an outside plant engineer."

My dates are building the Matrix.
    Wire framing.
        Subterranean fiberoptic paths.
            User experience design.

I smile at them.
"Wow, you make the Internet?"
    Because the Lexapro works
        and night is dark again.

                * * *

Because of Anne Boyer and Bertolt Brecht
Because of Stacy Szymaszek *Journals*.
Because of the low and ignoble
Because of the awful secrets

Because I date manically when my daughter
    lives with her father
        And yesterday I rode the subway six times
            G, A, E, C, L, L to meet men.

Because I want to see who is unhoused
    because I have tried in my twenty years as a New Yorker not to see

Because in my recurring panic attack nightmare that happens every week
    I don't have a home

Because this is one of the worst things that can happen in New York
Because the shelters are a joke

Because my dating is my attempt to ensure something dark and hard
    A man with an apartment, space for me, under the staircase even

Because the man on the E with a swollen ankle and a cane,
    asleep sitting up, who mumbled "Get away," when I stood too close

Because of the nest of blankets with a sleeping body underneath
    by the turnstile at the 42nd street A, C, E entrance

Because of the skater punk who sleeps in the park
    with a pit bull on a rope who smiled at me on 6th Avenue

Because I hate it when my students write about "homeless people"
    in Washington Square Park

Because some of the men are keeping their apartments for 23-year-old women

Because the Roman
    had a tattoo of several lines from *Fight Club* on his right forearm
        in Italian cursive

Because I ran my finger over it and he smiled

Because I wake up staring at an elderly cat's grizzled chin
Because my daughter has taken to calling him, "soldier cat
    because he is serious and grouchy"

Because he said there is something wrong with Rome
    and I nodded like I knew that too.

***

I wake up to essay prompt, poem, and lesson plan

Suspension of punctuation

I want to keep the Passover workbook
    and throw away the plastic easter eggs.

I look up the word aura
    nimbus
        sensory stimulus

The woman I know who got into a cab drunk
    The man who pushed her in

And what happened next

She doesn't want to tell us the name of the bar

"Why do you want to know?" she asks. "Why?"

                * * *

She says, "We did so many chores we're like Cinderella."

We watch *Arrietty*, a movie about little people who live in drawers
    Borrowers of small things
        Sugar cube and safety pin
            There is a mother who worries her fears awake
                And a daughter who learns to fight

I skip the poetry conference like I always do
    and turn off my phone.

***

In the dream I disappoint my future in-laws
    who are living in Hong Kong

My boots are too American
I have too many stuffed animals
    and disrupt a ceremonial father-son painting session
        with questions about the train schedule

The cat wakes me up
    I chase him under the dining room table
        he scratches the tip of my ring finger

A prick for the girls at their looms
    spinning spinning

Tender finger, you suck

                  * * *

I've been approved to travel
    but this Google doc is a mess

At the faculty meeting with the alcoholic
    Orgasms are metaphors
        for revelations, for theory, for freewriting

Facebook says its sibling day
    I can't find a picture of us together
        Each parent took one kid
            Splitsville
            Poof

* * *

Alice Notley is in town
    which means I have limited access to her granddaughters

We will see *Home*
    a girl from Barbados, a fat cat, and an alien

The candidate teaches us about Benjamin
    and the Vietnamese way of thinking about copies
        model, mimic, real, and fake goods

I am left with aura,
    which my students say reminds them of Aurora,
        their favorite Disney princess

The aura withers and decays
The aura is the atmosphere about a goddess
Thunderhead

  see stop raining
    see April

         * * *

"No one cares about squirrels except you,"
  the woman says to her dog.

I will make some of my students
  write about the Kenyan students
    who were murdered

Do you know how to fix a razor scooter?

Do you know if that cheap camp is any good,
  the one at the settlement house?

Amy Poehler made me wish for a son,
  for a minute.

"You ain't bad, you ain't nothing," he sang
  and we loved him for it.

When I stop in the street to write poems on my phone,
  the people sigh.

I am in the way of all commerce, like most poets

The dog I had for one beaten year
  scratched my *Thriller* album

I cried the tears of the lost things

Ours was not a house of replacements

You lost it

You lost it

I'm lucky enough to find this bench

I want my animals to take care of me,
    like in Cinderella

Some of us are already naked in the park

* * *

He made the crawl space underneath the stairs
    into a fort

He rolled himself up in the blanket before sleeping
    we called it "the burrito"

The beer can evidence in the backyard when
    the snow melted

"He's drinking again," she said, he said, they always say that

"I let them beat me with trees."

I like to kiss my dates next to the asbestos dumpster
    on 3rd street
        close to my apartment, but not too close

"I just want to have fun," says my laptop.

The list says:
shampoo
conditioner
hunk of cheddar
O.J.
Bread

Are you ready to chaperone?

                          * * *

So what if I'm distracted?
So what if I'm overwhelmed?
So what if yesterday when a student asked me to repeat what I'd just said,
    I whispered, "No, I'm sorry, I just can't."

It's April 17th and my ex and I owe $9000 in taxes
    and still I keep writing poems.

Yesterday on the walk to school, I saw a cast-off belt
    in the middle of the sidewalk.
"Snake!" my heart said and we walked around it
    like we were on a mountain trail
        like we were somewhere else

I remembered Reese Witherspoon playing Cheryl Strayed
    in *Wild*—a rattler on her path, that shaking leg, eyeing the ground, side-step—
        and that I've become addicted to the *Dear Sugar*
           podcast on polyamory

keep a couple of boyfriends in every borough

more Don Draper than Peggy, Betty, or Joan

working on not being grouchy in the mornings
    So far, I have only managed to receive half of a check mark.

"Your hair is too short," she says.
    "You look just like a boy."

* * *

The radio says coconut oil is over-hyped as a curative
    A migrant boat capsized en route from Libya to Italy
        950 on the boat, only 28 rescued

I am going to teach the hell out of that white fragility essay

I remember how I cried after my Caribbean literature class
    sophomore year because for once in school
        a professor made me not matter

Later I'd go to graduate school and get used to that
    become invisible and sniveling outside of office hours
        with a soft egg of an idea about *Jane Eyre* or *Romeo and Juliet*

Last night in bed I read Michael Broder's *This Life Now*
    and this morning, still in the nest of my duvet, I listened to R. Erica Doyle
        reading from *Proxy* at the Poetry Project.

Tony
The boardwalk
Sweeping the hair from his mom's salon floor
The ghosts on NYC streets
Flu that is a virus
Jason and Buffy
Dreams of soft and hard fucking
You see the thing is

The Marquis de Sade at 6
The deferential equation
No child left behind
The way women are so polite
The second person, the you, the you, the you
The stupid birth control pills
Days of soft and hard fucking
Erica Kaufman giggling in the audience

* * *

I am to think
   of the poem as a
      series of ships.

I am to think I have sailed.

She says, "I'll be your girlfriend,"
    when I say I don't have a boyfriend.

He had a nice apartment.
That one bought me a French press
   and still I left.

The clothes that come in the mail do not fit.

April, you windy torn sail,
   will you be my voyage out
      and carry me to summer on deck?

Navigate past that black deep whorl some say is a monster?

If you think of a poem as a ship,
   maybe you won't expect it to land.

* * *

Last night on Netflix
   Zizek told me to
      change my dreams

And so instead there was a reading
   where the poets danced.

Kind of like the *Thriller* video, but messier.
Kind of like what I imagine Julian
   doing at his powwow dance class.
      And I missed Julian
         and got sad about Nick.

It was his journal and I was just a girl
   who looked good dancing.

* * *

My job is to hold the sadness
   in tea cups and tote bags

   while you rip up the floor
     with your razor scooter.

Your job is to go to bed.

My job is to act like a ship on the lip of your tears.
  To ride you out,
    to surf you,
      to sail.

Your job is to what?

* * *

At Lenny's I order a baconeggandcheese
  The woman behind the counter
    knows my name
      small glee
Now maybe we can talk about shit

I re-read Charlie LeDuff's essay "What Killed Aiyana-Stanley Jones" and
   then I stop
  for five minutes to stare at the police officers next to me
    I am trying to cry
      I am trying not to cry

I am afraid of them
  but one of them is hot in a gym way

I leave to teach
  There is a woman in the corner, maybe 50, with a mullet
    and two stacks of cassette tapes in front of her

On 8th street from the one remaining bong store
    Whitney Houston
        "Oh, I wanna dance with somebody
            I wanna feel the heat with somebody"

I am that girl again
    that little ankle kick step she did
Hope, hope, hope
    I waited by the T.V. for the top-of-the-hour hit video
Whitney all gospel and pop
Before the blow
Before Bobby

* * *

What does April mean?
That some of us are dying in the midst of the ground—
    bulbs, seeds, buds, insects—coming back to life.

She says, "All animals hibernate, even lions."

I write messages to the faces, but different faces write back.
Ants stitch the seam of my kitchen floor.

The Spaniards take over the Japanese café.
    Chatty in their sportswear.
        I keep writing.
            Don't look up.
                Give the man a dollar.

Once I was a girl who studied away.
I have tried to use my body as a way to gather knowledge.

How many bodies are too many?
How much cake is too much?

The phone says, "I'm thinking we never see each other in person."

Last night all three of us were in the bathroom.
    The baby, the bathwater.
Did we throw it all out?
Why yes, we did.

The email about spiders in my eyes.
What are the things we are not talking about?

* * *

10,000 march
peacefully
in Baltimore
Caitlin Jenner on T.V.
Aftershock in Nepal

Couples' therapy
    all around

I like this man
I don't like this man
Swipe through
Swipe through

April is a lamb now
Shoe panic!

I sleep with the wolf
    again
His is an animal joy

The bed is a vista
    horizon
        of shoulders
and ass.
    Legs.

Everything lately
    is a wave,
a howdy,
a shoehorn
to get us to May.

I suppose
the lamb is for
    Jesus.

Oh wait,
    that's March,
says my phone.

April is about
    showers,
        flowers.

But I'm stuck on
    lions,
    lambs,
    wolves.

And lambchop,
    that sweet puppet.

* * *

Berthold Brecht wrote "Poets are to tell the truth."
    But we have to be keen and cunning.
        And there is capitalism
            Slaughter and stink.

April is the month of poetry.
    Some of us write every day, but most of us can't.

And what if the poem is just a passing through?
    Transport and portal.
        Deep space.
            Sidewalk chalk.
                The long commute.

The images I Google of portals are neon
    Fiery and mirrored
        Cosmic rope bridge
            Alien highway

I stand at the mouth of May
    I flip my paper Staples wall calendar
        Step through
            Step through

III.
FUTURE PERFECT

Lexapro Poem

You're tripping or
you're pregnant or
you're dizzy or
you're giddy or
you're slipping or

Someone else is driving
your bumper car
crash crash

You're hilarious now or
Your writing is so honest

You cuddle with your kid
for way longer
because late is not a category
and school is not a place

This upward facing dog is a riff
This corner is all, "Walk, Walk, Walk"
This trashcan is 100% banana peel
Those shoes are a must
That coffee takes all of the cream
Those men will all get messages in their inboxes
These trees are green, green, green.

Future Perfect

My future ex-husband arrives late to the haunted mansion.
    He carries a fancy cutting board under his arm.
        The dream me made bread.
        "I'm worried about you," he whispers into my neck, but he won't stay.

My future ex-husband and I leave the bar.
    The last call lights made us sheepish and stunned.
        We stand in a blizzard and stare at a banker who barfs on a snow bank.

My future ex-husband and I text fight about Duran Duran.
    He floats away from me at tripping speed on a puffy hand-drawn rain cloud.
        His muscled thighs, dyed auburn hair, and lip gloss
            make him the technicolored star of his own movie.

My future ex-husband is a wolf.
    He invites me back to his workshop by which he means lair
        by which he means room with no heat by which he means cave.

My future ex-wife wears yellow chiffon to the frat house dinner party.
    She's petite like baby dolls and hop-hop-hopping sparrows.
        During the pre-dinner cheese and champagne buffet, I squeeze her
        and she squirms away.

My future ex-wife is the surgically enhanced robot servant version of me.
    Bigger tits.
        Poutier lips.
            Wittier tweets.

My future-ex-wife is an avatar or an app or fembot or a troll,
    anonymously hacking all of the married computers and doxing
        the husbands' Citibank savings accounts.

My future ex-person is that baby over there, howling on the A train.
    Hungry for pretzels.
        Hot in a Polo Christmas sweater.

My future ex-wife is so pretty she'll bust your heart.
    Like a pageant wave.
        Like a bikini bottom.

My future ex-wife pickles in her roof top garden.
    She's a collaborative grant writer who loves to snuggle.
        She's my "partner-in-crime."
            We collect shells in the in low-tide sun.

My future ex-wife is that $1500 purse and the bar where you don't belong.
    She's the neon eyes in the loft windows near the Williamsburg Bridge.
        Horizon vision.
            Beer googles.
                Night glasses.

Have you seen my future ex-person?
    I lost them at the upstate mall.
        I left them at the touristy taco stand in Tulum or a sea monster ate them.
            How did they get away?

Winter Wonderland

All of the parents are single.

I watch the fifth graders dance.
    The boys shove.
        The girls wear pumps and carry small purses.

I remember what Freud said about reticules
    and I Shazam three songs.

She says I'm not looking at her enough.
    Later, she gets a crown of ice-blue flowers
        painted onto her forehead.

At midnight, my phone says, "Sneak off and come to HiFi."
    And then, "Okay, fine, don't."

"Duh," I say back to it. "Just duh."

Mourning Instructions

To flatten your heart
   open a window.
Or lie on your back
   next to a wolf.

The thing about girls and women
   is that they disappear and sometimes come back pregnant.

The article says, "214 of the 234 Nigerian schoolgirls,"
   and you weigh the options: raped and alive, home instead of away.

To flatten your feet
   try breathing.
Or whisper the word "Change,"
   while you remember your kid tugging at the string of your arm
     or that casual fuck
     or a needle floating in the fountain.

To wonder about the girls you had given up on,
   look out the window and squint until you get a headache

My Second Husband

A tall man from Chicago tricks me into marrying him.

"Technically, I'm still someone else's wife," I worry at his aunt, a teacher like me.
    "And my kid isn't here. I can't do this without my kid."
The aunt shrugs.
    "It's too late. The caterers have arrived."

I watch the wedding cellist.
    Her gray case splayed open on the chemically green lawn.
        She runs the bow along her forearm.

My groom waits for me in a gazebo.
    He whispers into my neck, "It'll make my parents happy.

Apology

Your future-ex-husband lives in the Parthenon.
    Inside, his girlfriend has set up a makeshift gallery.
        She's sculpted a marble cabin out of mottled pink stone.

The sign says, "Group show."
    You knock and surprise them on the bed.
        Back out, "Sorry, sorry."

In the morning the siren starts and stops.
    Rain on the roof.
        A cross on the horizon.
            Bed Stuy's full gray sky.

You trip on the broken sidewalk.
    There's yarn stitched into a chain-link fence and a girl with a paw for a hand.

Once there was a mouse in a glue trap.
    Two back feet stuck.

You both knew he'd gnaw them off to get away,
    so you shut the pantry door.

Do You Have a Boyfriend?

The radio plays a show on solitaries.
   "Monks are big drinkers," it says.
      But we are not talking about hermits.

If I put my heart on ice, I can carry it around in an Igloo cooler for the
      next warm body.

This medicine is hard to take.
   We feel the chill of forty-one degrees in March after the first warm day
      of spring.

If I put my heart in a plastic bag
   like the goldfish at the PetSmart,
      later, we can find a suitable tank.

The wolf kept a heap of rotting hearts underneath the staircase,
   the space where we joked would be her bedroom.
      He nosed them.
         Blood on a wet muzzle.

"Do you have a boyfriend?"
   She raspberried my face and I wiped the spit off my glasses.

Lion or Lamb

The sunlight bumps up against my eyes
    and I want to be crated like the blind puppy
        I know myself to be.

Squint. Squint.
    March doesn't know shit about April.

I can't get through to the woman who runs the bagel shop.
    "I am open."
        I repeat, "I am open.
            Unless I change my mind about the level of openness. Okay?"

My queer boyfriend has a lot of laundry,
    which I am not allowed to fold.

The drunk white man dances in front of the semi on Metropolitan.
    "What do you know? What do you know?" he sings until the police van
        comes.

Hard talks stoned are still hard talks.

My phone says, "We lost the twins and I'm ready for a girlfriend

Early Morning

My back is a bag of knees.

Sometimes the anxiety breaks through the Lexapro and I wake up at four a.m.

I leave the bed.
   I check my OkCupid messages.
     "Hey shortygirl.
       Meet for a drink?

"Mama!"
   she yells.

I go in and lie down again.
"Big beetles," she says.
   "Are not real," I answer and rub her back.
     I go back to the couch.

Teaching presentation.
Copies.

Scroll through Vanessa Place thread.
Scroll through kids in poems thread.
Scroll through Alice Neel paintings thread.

Read Ruth Ellen Kocher letter.
Read *Huffington Post* article about the history of mapping the clitoris.
Read *Jezebel* article about the journalist trying to discredit Emma Sulkowicz.

Get up.
Feed cat.
Take bath.
Pack lunch.

Frankincense

The poet doesn't know I'm a poet.
    At the dinner party
        on rainy 8th Avenue in Brooklyn, she says
"Where have you been?
    I don't see you at readings.
        Just at the co-op."

I will smoke it if you roll it.

Gender is boring.
    I am questioning, questing, quitting.

May is for confusion and grading.

Drunk as usual on the G train.
    Starring at the phantom hand that strokes
        the ponytail of the woman with the iced Starbucks drink
            and silver Birkenstocks.

You with your sneakers.
    H who kept ordering the drinks
        and put shea butter and frankincense on you before the transfer.

"It's okay," she said. "I see you."

Mother's Day Poem

My mother visits this weekend.
    "Do you want me to help you clean?"

I am ignoring her to write this poem.
    There are fairies shouting on the TV.
        I take a Midol and 4 ibuprofen.

"Did you run the dishwasher?
    Can we do a load of laundry?
        I don't have any more underwear."

We watch the new Netflix documentary about the star chefs.
    Quail eggs encrusted in ash.
        King crab in almost burnt cream.
            Pig's head in sourdough, pickled gooseberry, tarragon salt.

"The food is like art," we say.

Later in a dream, I meet the Pope
    and he serves me ambrosia from a nonstick pan.

It tastes like store-bought blueberry pie.
    Chemical slick on the roof of my mouth.
        I feel miffed.
        I expected Zeus's ecstasy or Hera's MDMA.

As a girl I ate my grandma's Jello salads.
    Sea foam and strawberry ribbon were my favorites.

I never liked the one called ambrosia,
    made with marshmallows, cool whip, and coconut flakes.

Quickie

I watch the Syrian refugees crawl under a barbed-wire fence.
    A backpack snags.
        I close the computer.

Finland says they will take 30,000 and the prime minister offers up his
    country home.

For an hour I have 80 students in my apartment.
    I stand on a chair to talk to them.
        Their excitement rubs off on me and turns the day
            into something I can do.

At night I dream an entire relationship from first date to break up.
    He's a dad and a speed freak.
        We get drunk, fuck, have brunch
            and then he tells me he's moving to Ireland.

I watch him pack while I text my disapproving friends.
    He leaves me with his kid, who is playing video games in the other
    room.
        Eventually, his mother comes.
            "This always happens," she says to me and takes her kid.

I stand in his empty apartment.
The white walls are darker where the posters used to hang.

I am halving the pills.
    Weaning myself.

Come back dreams.

Come back smaller woman who lives inside of bloated woman.

Mediation

We meet in Stacy's apartment.
    Is it a poetry retreat?
        Or maybe she asked us to paint her walls?

Everyone knows we are still good at working together.

A canvas on the wall.
    Maybe Brainard's *Pansies* or one of Rothko's blues.

We sit and write about the painting.
This is a new kind of dream.
One without longing.
    Just work.

We make fun of the mediator.
Just like we did with the therapist.

"Are you sure this is the right thing?
Clearly you have great affection for one another."

The documents are from another era.
    Plaintiff.
    Defendant.
    The rights we waive.

We rush through so that there's time for dim sum

Specimen

Sometimes I imagine my frozen embryos in midtown accidentally thawing.
Sometimes I take my heart out of the cooler and watch its veins redden,
    quick with blood.

In *Star Wars,* we learned that you can freeze a whole person.
    Like leftovers.
    Like in my mother's garage meat freezer.
        Full of venison and whole chickens.

Are you ready for the apocalypse? she thinks, but doesn't say.

Han Solo writhes and twists.
    It hurts to thaw!
He's temporarily blind.
Thank god for Chewie.

I imagine the little blast of cells from a photo the doctor once gave me.
"That's in you," he said and then asked me if I thought his son would get
        into NYU.
    "We'll freeze the rest."

I am to decide what?
The aura of the cells is more powerful than the actual cells.

I am asking you to wither and decay.
Will you?
Can you?

My Coven

Before the evaluations I laughed too hard and said,
    "I'm becoming a bruja!"
Because of the locally-sourced coffee and the new feminism.

They gave me a necklace that looked like a cookie.
    Two sprinkled hearts, co-joined, eating each other, and in cursive,
        Riots Not Diets.

One of them came out
    while we made zines, listened to my best Spotify mix,
        blogged, and read the texts.
            The Halberstam.
        The Moten.
            The Preciado.

The computer says, "Que te joden, bruja"

In Madrid, the word fuck, its layers
    No te jode
    Es un libro jodido
    Que se joda

S teaches me how to use a necklace to see if my chakras are open or closed.
    Root open.
    Gut open.
    Heart closed.
    Throat open.
    Third eye closed.
    Crown open.

G writing her horoscopes next to me at the Bed Stuy café where they serve
    wine.

Is that dick pic photographer video real or a joke?

At the witchcraft store called *Enchantments* I buy all of the pre-made road-opening
  spells because my plan is all horizon, total vista.

My trouble is with the present, not the future.

I order the self-help book about being single.
   The one with the research in it.
     I order the memoir from the divorced man about online dating.

A couple of my students are getting paid for their writing.

I pitch and pitch and pitch.

Post Bowie

My profile says I'm a feminist dreamer
    who loves kale cocktails, clams on pizza, bears, and film nerds.

I might be too nice for this shit.
His bedroom made me sad.
Quit your dreaming.

The jobs where I've been fired for spacing out and refusing to tuck in my
    shirt.

Turns out we have a lot of feelings about David Bowie and his make-up
    artists.
    I can name queerer misfits, but I won't.

I don't let the futures sleep over.
    Because of the after shave.
    Because of my insomnia.
    Because I can't re-shape the air if they are sucking it up.

We can't have indictments, but a couple of them will lose their jobs.
    Sniff. Sniff.

I confess here that I fluffed up the dreams
    or I traded them in
        or I pimped them out.

Because arbitrage is seductive.
    Trade your fat for sleep!
    Trade your night for morning!

Trade gurl for boi!
Trade present body for future self!

Rituals for Saying Good-Bye to Things that Never Quite Were

The scientist on the phone describes the band of cells.
"In taking it, the embryo is destroyed."

"Are you okay with that?" he asks.
Yes.
I think so.

The bank where the cells will live and replicate is more utopian than
HSBC or Chase
because there are unlimited withdrawals.

Consider the lost boy.
The horizon receding through the dusty back windshield.
A blue plastic suitcase splayed open in the middle of the road.
A torn sundress whipping off the antennae.

Your California life.
Your other babies.
That one perfect husband.

The computer says:
Burn it.
Give it to the wind.
Let it float away.
Make a ceremony.
Clear space in your house.

Once there was a photograph of my mother:
Scarf in her hair

    Strong legs
    On a bike
    Off and away
    Vista
    Gone
    A woman I never met
    My other mother

"Are you okay with that?"
    Yes.
        I think so.

My phone chirps, "Tincture of weed."

I will try a poem ritual, the crystal store on 10th Street, a pre-made spell, and Conrad's somatics.

Whatever it takes to cue the future.

Heart Less

My dumb heart thinks it knows something,
    but really its tick is all flounder and worry, wallow and sorry.
A wall of it.
A waterfall of it.
Caterwaul and carnival.
Container ship and Holland Tunnel.
It's a vessel with a bad idea.
Fat and slinking.
A car bomb.
A booty text.
Too many DJ requests.

Once it wanted a baby.
Another time it snuck out for a steak.
I try my best to slow it,
    talk it down,
        beat it back,
            eat it out.

But eventually I give up.
I take her out, my specimen, my lover.
And when we get to the bar, I put her in the pickle jar on the counter.
I play a country song about a bad marriage and an old farmhouse
    on the jukebox.
I shrug when the other customers point at her.
"No idea," I mouth and then pucker my lips in mock sympathy.
And then I go into the bathroom to dance alone.

ACKNOWLEDGEMENTS

Many thanks to the editors and staff of the following journals for publishing these poems:

Bone Banquet, "Transplant"
Brooklyn Rail, "Future Perfect," "Pushy," and "Tender Hooks"
Literary Mama, "My Pretty"
Mom Egg Review, "Code"
Tinderbox, "The Fisherman's Wife" and "Parachute"
The Women's Studies Quarterly, "Proxy"

And to Dancing Girl Press for publishing "Portal Poem" in their chapbook series.

I am indebted and so very grateful to Michael Broder and Indolent Books for choosing *Heart Less* for publication, and for creating a press whose mission is, among other things, to publish poets over fifty without a first poetry collection. Thank you Michael for seeing us, and championing our work. Without you, this book wouldn't exist.

I'd like to thank my poetry teachers: Ruth Stone, Milton Kessler, Liz Rosenberg, Marilyn Nelson, Phil Levine, Sharon Olds, Galway Kinnell, and William Matthews.

Thank you to Camille Guthrie, Daniel Nester, and Stacy Szymaszek for your brilliant and heartfelt blurbs. Special extra thanks to Dan for always believing in my work and that someday I would have a first book of poetry.

Thank you to all of my friends and chosen family who love and support me. In no particular order, Jason Nunes, Elke Dehner, Joelle Hann, Amy

Shearn, Philip Kain, Madeleine George, Lisa Kron, Megan Milks, James Polchin, Lynn Melnick, Amy Touchette, Smoota, Stephanie Hopkins, Dawn Lundy Martin, Suzanne Menghraj, Meghan Scibona, Arielle Greenberg, Mike Simone, Bill Martin, Bill Webb, Joe Vallese, and Rosa Mazzurco. If I've forgotten anyone, I'm sorry. I am lucky to have such chosen family in my life.

I am not sure I'd have kept writing poetry if it weren't for the steady friendship and support of Matt Longabucco.

Malka Longabucco, you are the poetry in my every day.

ABOUT THE AUTHOR

Carley Moore is a queer, disabled writer who has published two novels, *Panpocalypse* (Feminist Press, 2022) and *The Not Wives* (Feminist Press, 2019); an essay collection, *16 Pills* (Tinderbox Editions, 2018); a poetry chapbook, *Portal Poem* (Dancing Girl Press, 2016; and a young adult novel, *The Stalker Chronicles* (Farrar, Straus, and Giroux, 2011). *Heart Less* is her debut poetry book. Her work has appeared in *Aster(ix), The American Poetry Review, Book Forum, Electric Literature, Lit Hub,* and *The Los Angeles Review of Books.* Carley received a Best of the Net Award in Non-Fiction for her essay "My Big Gay Essay" and an Indie Foreword Award for her novel *The Not Wives*. *The Not Wives* was also a finalist for a Lambda Literary Award for Bisexual Fiction and a Firecracker Literary Award. Her novel *Panpocalypse* was a finalist for the Brooklyn Public Library's Literary Prize and the American Library Association Stonewall Book Award-Barbara Gittings Literature Award. Edition Assemblage published the German translation of *Panpokalypse* in March 2024. Carley is a Clinical Professor of Writing and Creative Production at New York University and an Associate at The Institute for Writing and Thinking at Bard College where she works with teachers across disciplines and grade levels to use more writing in the classroom. She lives with her daughter and two cats in Brooklyn. You can find her on Instagram @fragmentedsky or blogging on Substack.

ABOUT INDOLENT BOOKS

Founded in 2015 as a home for poets over 50 without a first book, Indolent Books today publishes innovative, provocative, and risky books by a diverse and inclusive range of writers across genres.

www.ingramcontent.com/pod-product-compliance
Lightning Source LLC
Chambersburg PA
CBHW060538080526
44586CB00012B/791